SCIENCE
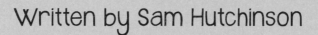
ACTIVITY
Book

Written by Sam Hutchinson

Designed and illustrated by
Vicky Barker

FOR
YOUNG
READERS

WHAT IS SCIENCE?

Science is more than bubbling liquids and test tubes. Science is about trying to understand the world around us, learning from it and using that information in the future. This information comes from experiments that have to follow strict rules so that the results can be trusted. Without strong evidence, someone's idea is just an idea and not a scientific fact.

WHAT IS STEM?

STEM stands for "science, technology, engineering and mathematics." These four areas are closely linked, and engineers couldn't do their jobs without science, technology or math. Math and science are the tools that engineers use to solve problems and create machines. Engineers pay attention to new discoveries in science as inspiration for new tools they can use to solve problems in ways that hadn't been possible before.

         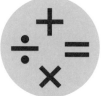

Science   Technology   Engineering   Math

OBSERVING ODDITIES

Top scientists use big words to describe their observations properly. They will use words like **OPAQUE** (you cannot see through it) or **TRANSPARENT** (you can see through it) so we know exactly what they are looking at.

Can you spot the objects on these scientists' benches that match the descriptions below?

1. The liquid was very bright, colorful and **opaque**.

2. The hammer was made from a very **bendy** material.

3. The girl's scarf was very **stiff** and difficult to wear.

4. The wrapping paper was **transparent** so I could see the present inside.

5. The cushion was made from a very **rough** material so it was uncomfortable to sit on.

(Answers at the back of the book.)

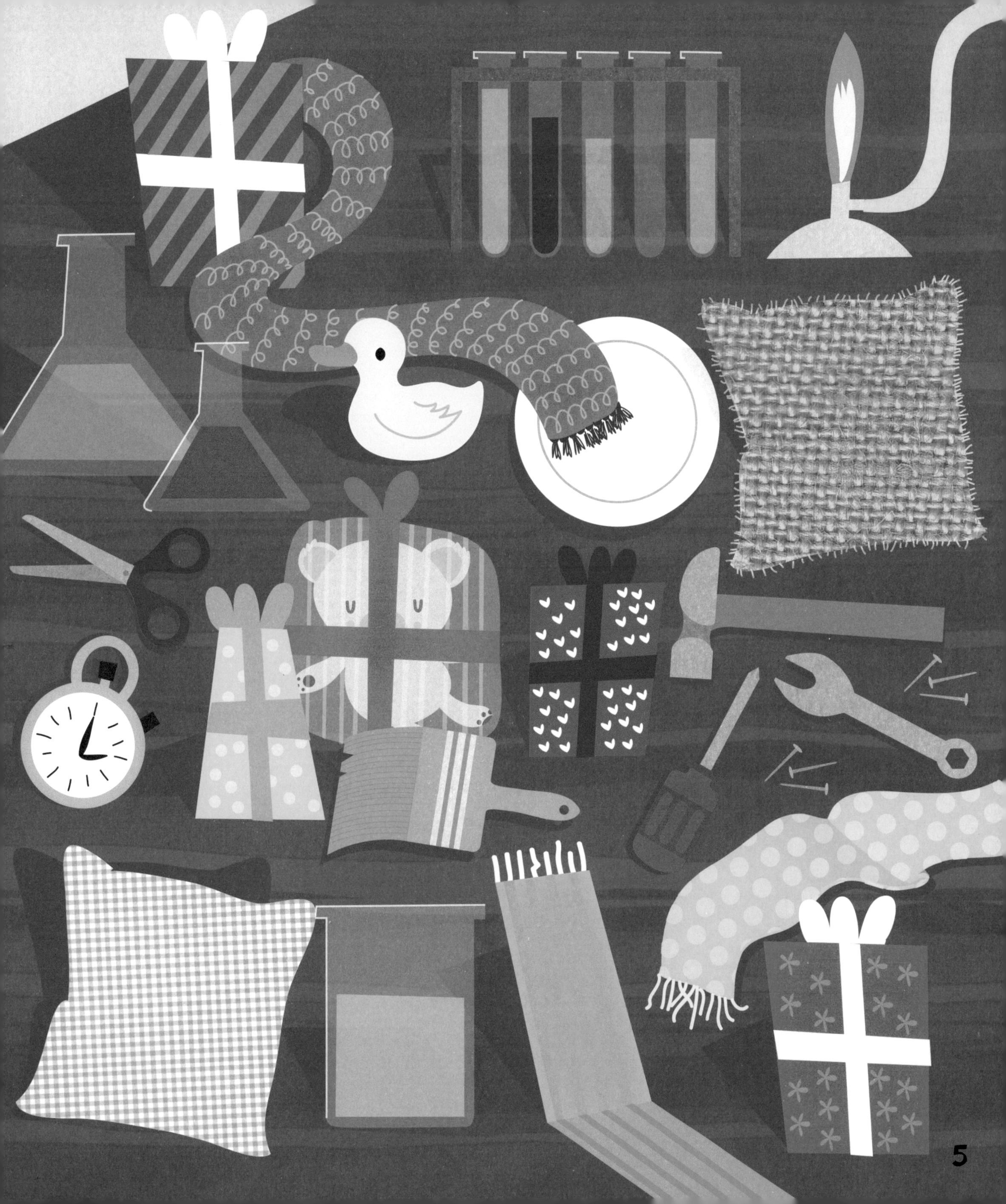

TWIST AND SHOUT

Materials that objects are made from have their own characteristics. These characteristics are a bit like their personality and help us to decide what to use them for. For example, some materials are very easy to squash or squish or twist and other materials are very hard to squash or squish or twist.

Chair made of wood

Imagine that this person is sitting on a chair made from different materials. Look at the labels and draw the chairs!

Chair made of sponge

Chair made of stone

Inflated beach ball chair

Chair made of cake

CHANGING STATE

The characteristics of a material can change.
Water becomes snow or ice under **0 degrees Celsius** and it
becomes steam very quickly over **100 degrees Celsius.**

Draw this glass of water
(with lemon wedge to make
it fancy!) next to the
temperatures below.
What state will the water be in?

(Answers on page 30.)

ICE   WATER   STEAM

°**C** = degrees Celsius

°**F** = degrees Fahrenheit

-10°C / 14°F

35°C / 95°F

18°C / 64.4°F

101°C / 213.8°F

TURNING TURBINES

The turbines in power plants spin to create electricity. The people who run power plants use different ways to make the turbines spin but the most popular method is to use steam. You will see on the following pages the different ways of creating steam in power plants.

The electricity generated by the turbines then travels along power cables to your home and gives power to your electrical devices.

STEAM

Start

Find your way through this maze as steam helps create electricity.

(Answer on page 30.)

Turbine

OLD ENERGY

Coal, gas and oil are made from plants and animals that died a long time ago and have been buried under soil and rocks ever since. Once these fuels have been burnt to make steam in power plants they cannot be used again. They create pollution that harms the environment.

Spot 10 differences between these scenes showing oil reserves at the bottom of the sea.

(Answers on page 30.)

10

NEW ENERGY

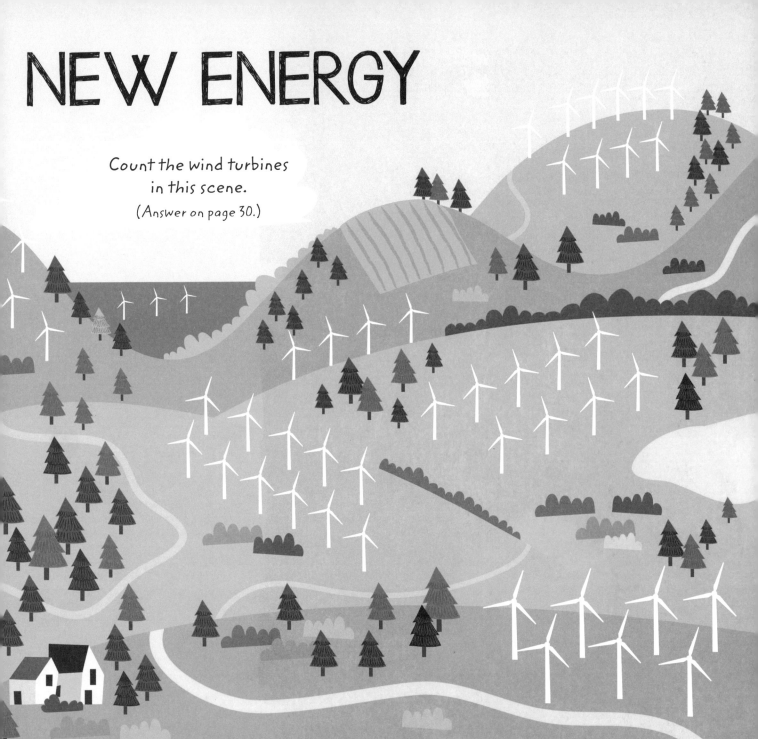

Count the wind turbines
in this scene.
(Answer on page 30.)

Wind turbines and hydro dams (hydro means "water" in ancient Greek) use wind or water, instead of steam, to make the turbines in a power station turn. Wind and water are called "green energy" because they can be used again and again. This is good for the environment. Some people do not like wind turbines and dams because they change the countryside.

SUN POWER

Solar panels (solar comes from the Latin for "sun") create heat from the sun's energy. This sort of energy is popular because it does not cause pollution or damage the countryside. You need a lot of space and a lot of sun to make enough energy from solar panels.

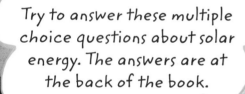

Try to answer these multiple choice questions about solar energy. The answers are at the back of the book.

1. SOLAR POWER PROVIDES A LARGE AMOUNT OF THE WORLD'S ENERGY.

a) TRUE
b) FALSE

2. WHICH OF THESE EXPLORER'S VEHICLES COMMONLY USES SOLAR POWER TO CREATE ENERGY?

a) SUBMARINE
b) SPACECRAFT
c) HELICOPTER
d) MOTORBIKE

3. ONE OF THE BIGGEST BENEFITS OF USING SOLAR POWER IS:

a) THE PROCESS DOES NOT CREATE MUCH POLLUTION.
b) THE SOLAR PANELS LOOK COOL.
c) YOU CAN BOAST ABOUT THEM TO YOUR FRIENDS.

4. WHICH OF THESE LOCATIONS ALREADY HAS SEVERAL LARGE-SCALE SOLAR POWER PLANTS?

a) WALES, UK
b) SIBERIA, RUSSIA
c) CALIFORNIA, USA

5. SOLAR POWER COMES DIRECTLY FROM SUNLIGHT. THE SUN IS:

a) A STAR
b) A PLANET
c) A GALAXY

NEW AND NUCLEAR

Nuclear reactors split atoms in order to generate the heat that turns water into steam which then turns turbines just like in other power plants. Atoms are made of smaller particles called protons, neutrons and electrons. Scientists fire neutrons at uranium atoms to split them, releasing more neutrons and energy. The process continues and is called a chain reaction. Nuclear reactions do not use fossil fuels but do create radioactive waste which is very harmful to humans and other creatures.

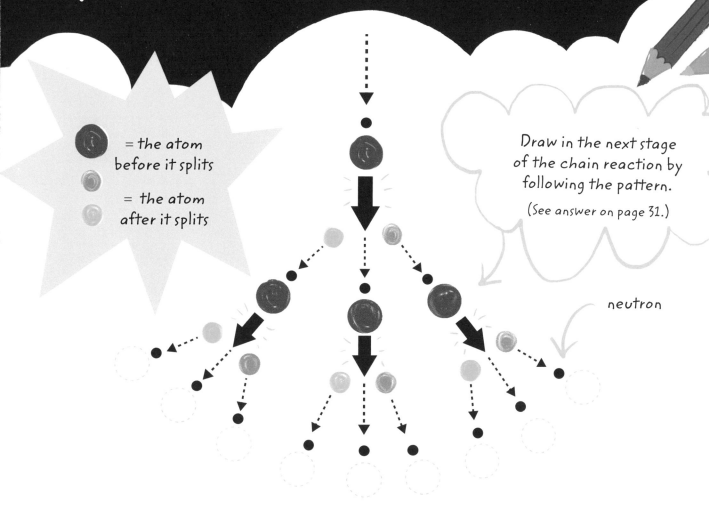

= the atom before it splits

= the atom after it splits

Draw in the next stage of the chain reaction by following the pattern.

(See answer on page 31.)

neutron

POSITIVES AND NEGATIVES

The circuit on this page has just been connected to light up the bulb.

Electrons are like little packets of electricity and they like to travel from the negative side of a battery to the positive side. Batteries were designed to make the most of this!

Draw in the electrons running from one side to the other illuminating the light bulb as they go.

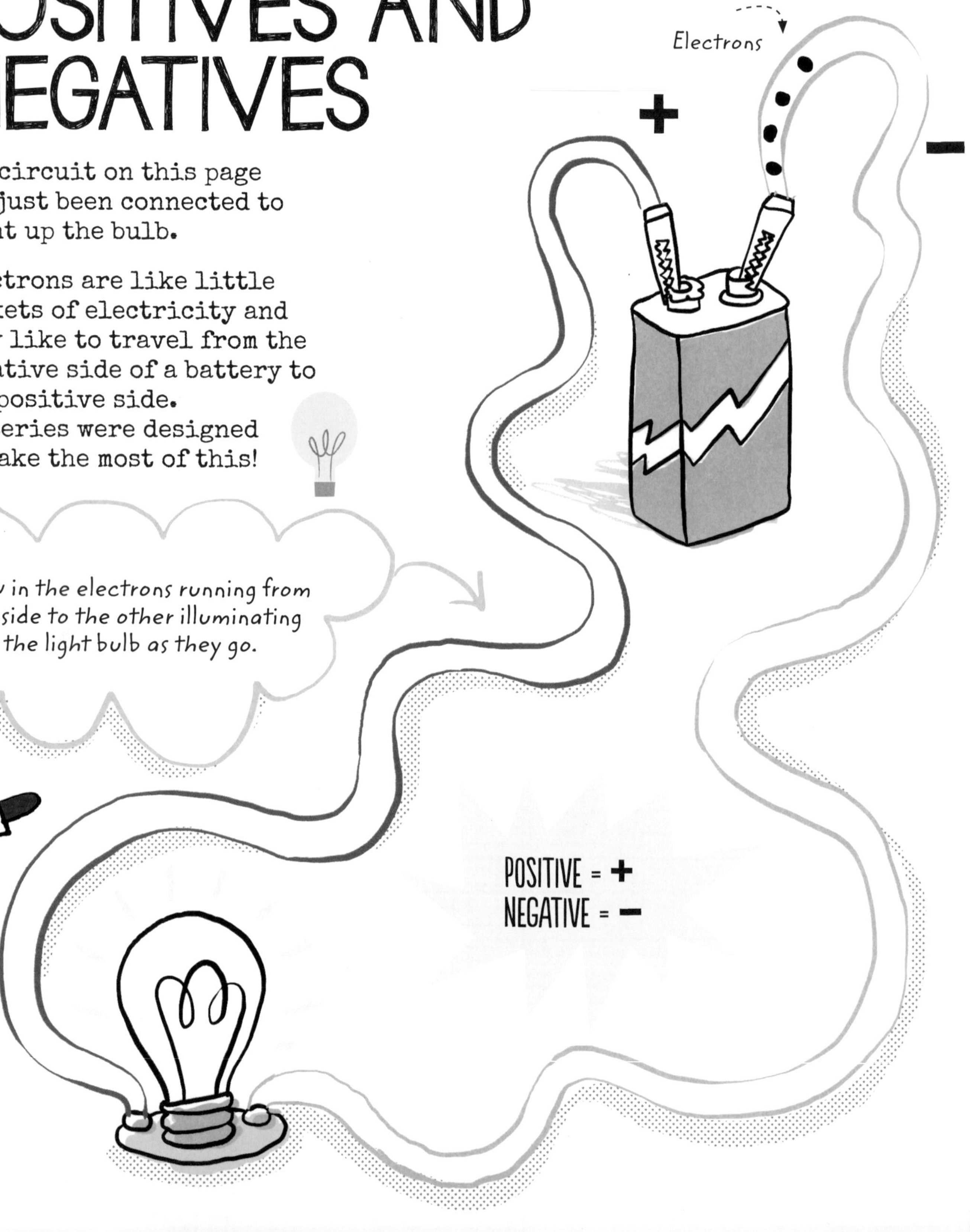

Electrons

+

−

POSITIVE = +
NEGATIVE = −

Find the electrically charged words in this word search.

```
f w z b k y i q u h j p o m b c v
e l e c t r i r u t n e g a t z w
h h b n e u t r o n d j k s m w j
d w r s x c v b n t r e t t c e g
g n e g e f x v t h c j m a e v e
h w a t l k a a a t o h k o h i v
j k r t e d w b r a s a a u k t m
k m m n c s a a m m p j n r n a n
l f n o t s t a t o m e k g g e
f h o p r q o t n e s h t o h e t
j k r l i e n e r q i c y n r n y
l p t m c i r c u i t l h w t h l
k p c m i h w s q m i p b a t h p
m w e y t r t b h j v o n h r t o
d a l r y p o i n t e u k m a g u
q r e w c g n e u t r a n r a n p
w t e g s t r m k l y r e t t a b
```

atom   charge   battery

neutron   positive   watt

electron   negative

electricity   circuit

Answers at the
back of the book.

STORMS OF ELECTRICITY

Thunder is the sound that lightning makes. You can hear thunder because your ears pick up the vibrations that lightning makes when it strikes. If the storm is close then you can see the lightning and hear the thunder almost at the same time. If the thunder follows a few seconds afterwards then the storm is further away and the vibrations have to travel further in order for you to hear them.

Lightning happens in the first place when small bits of ice bash into each other in a thundercloud creating positive and negative electric charges. As you saw on page 14, electricity travels between negative and positive charges. This electricity sparks between the two charges inside the clouds or, more rarely, sparks between the cloud and an object on the ground, such as a tree or a building. This is lightning.

Search in this scene for the following things:

- LIGHTNING FORK WITH FOUR PRONGS
- A FLOWER WITH SIX PETALS
- TWO RED UMBRELLAS
- A CAR WITH A BROKEN WINDOW
- THREE LITTLE BIRDS
- A CAT
- A TRACTOR
- A CUPCAKE

(Answers on page 31.)

WAVES OF SOUND

Sound waves are made by vibrations. The type of sound that you hear depends on the frequency and amplitude (size and height of the sound wave) and what the sound has to travel through to reach you.

Quieter

Louder

Higher pitch

Deeper pitch

Using the key, draw the sound waves to go with these sounds. The pitch is the type of sound.

(Answers on page 31.)

FIGHTER JET

LION'S ROAR

MOUSE'S SQUEAK

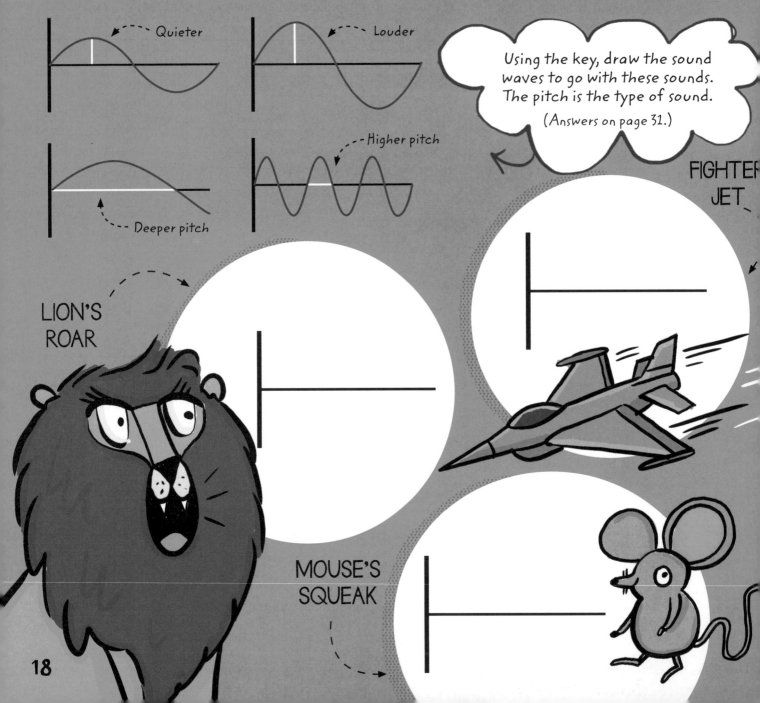

WHALE SONG

FART

ROCK CONCERT

YOU TALKING QUIETLY

YOU SHOUTING

19

SHADOW MAGIC

When there is something between an object and light then that thing casts a **shadow.**

The sun is our main source of natural light and during the day light reflects off objects and into our eyes so that we can see them. Darkness is the absence of light and this means that we cannot see what is around us. Shadows are examples of darkness that we can see.

Our shadow can be long and tall or short and small depending on where the sun is in the sky.

Match these dog owners with their pets using their shadows. Can you guess where the sun is coming from for each shadow? If so, add an arrow.

(See answers on page 32.)

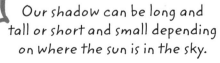

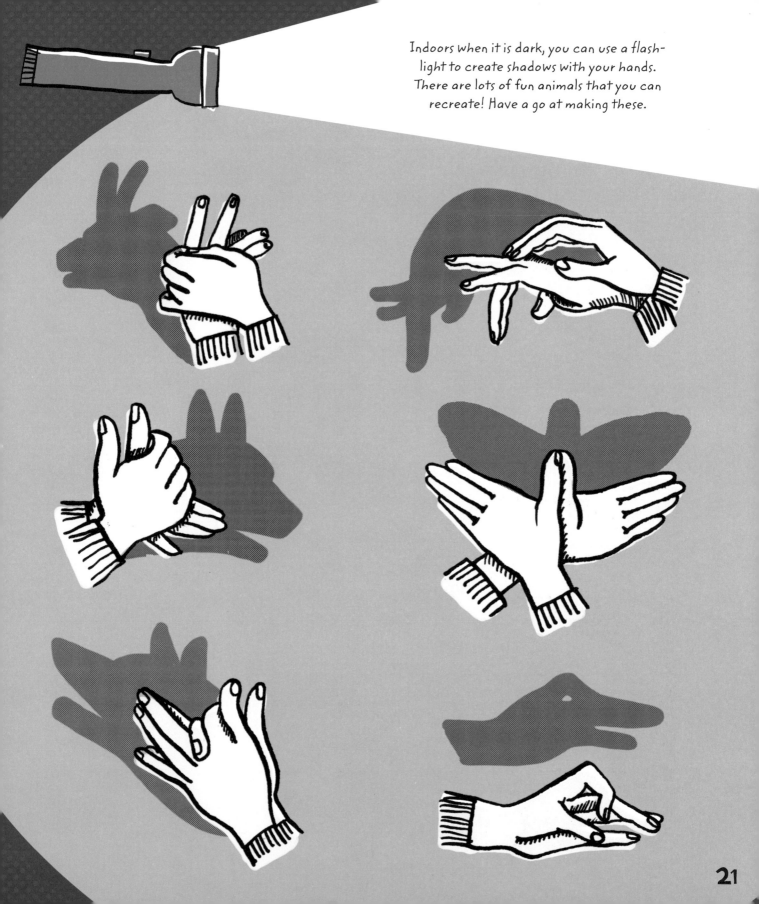

Indoors when it is dark, you can use a flashlight to create shadows with your hands. There are lots of fun animals that you can recreate! Have a go at making these.

WHAT A WHIFF!

Smells travel in the air. The smells are made up of chemicals. When you breathe them in, the chemicals tell your brain what you are smelling.

Choose what these people are smelling. Is it nice or is it nasty? Draw it in the thought bubbles.

GOOD TASTE

There are thousands of taste buds on your tongue. The food you eat reacts with the buds so that you can taste what you are eating.

Color in this picnic using the following key:

Sweet foods = red
Salty foods = blue
Sour foods = yellow
Bitter foods = green

(Answers on page 32.)

TOUCHING TRUTH

Touch a few things around you now. When you touch something, nerve endings in your skin send information to the brain. They tell you about temperature, how much something hurts and how much pressure you are feeling. Each part of your body communicates with its own part of the brain so that you know exactly where you are feeling something.

NAILS

ICE

RABBIT

JELLY

FIRE

Write down some words to describe how these things would feel if you touched them. Remember, never touch fire and be careful when touching other objects.

Fingerprints can be creative too!
Turn these prints into
little creatures.

OPPOSITES ATTRACT

Magnets attract metals that have iron in them, like steel and nickel. Materials such as wool, glass, wood or plastic are not magnetic. Magnets have a north pole and a south pole. The north pole will ATTRACT ➡️⬅️ south poles from other magnets but it will PUSH AWAY ⬅️➡️ north poles. The south pole attracts north poles and repels south poles.

Color the north poles of these bar magnets red and the south poles blue. You can tell which is which by looking at whether they are attracting each other or pushing each other away.

(Answers on page 32.)

= NORTH

= SOUTH

Imagine that you have thrown these things at the very strong magnet above the shark tank. Which ones will stick to the magnet and which ones will fall into the shark tank?
Draw them on the page.
See page 28 if you are not sure.

A SHEEP
A KEY
A T-SHIRT
A CAR
A FRIDGE MAGNET
A CAKE

(Answers on page 32.)

ANSWERS

Pages 4-5 ---->

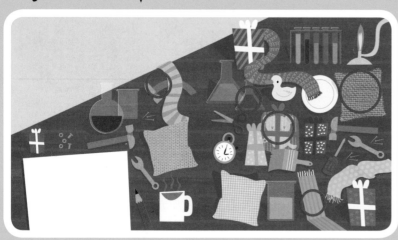

Page 8

-10°C	18°C	35°C	101°C
14°F	64.4°F	95°F	213.8°F
Ice	**Water**	**Water**	**Steam**

Page 9 ---->

Page 10 ---->

Page 11 ---->

There are **48** wind
turbines in the scene.

Page 12

1. b) False
2. b) Spacecraft
3. a) The process does not create much pollution
4. c) California, USA
5. a) A star

Page 13

Page 15

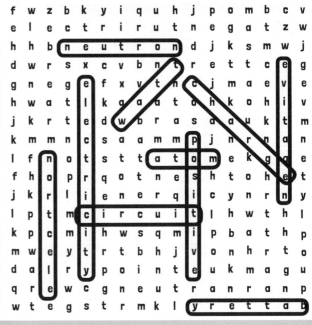

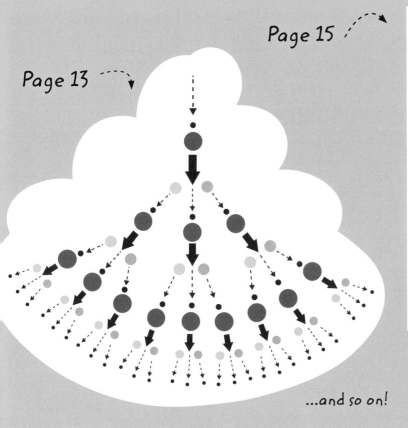

...and so on!

Pages 18-19

Pages 16-17

These answers just show the type of sound wave you can draw. So your one might look a bit different!

Page 20

Page 24

Page 25

Page 29

MAGNET:

a key
a car
a fridge magnet

SHARK TANK:

a sheep
a T-shirt
a cake

Page 28

How did you do?